P9-CSE-970

THE WORLD'S
MATERIAL
RESOURCES

Robin Kerrod

Thomson Learning
New York

First published in the United States in 1994 by
Thomson Learning, 115 Fifth Avenue, New York, NY 10003

First published in Great Britain in 1994 by
Wayland (Publishers) Ltd.

Library of Congress Cataloging-in-Publication Data
Kerrod, Robin.
  Material resources/Robin Kerrod.
     p.   cm.—(World's resources)
  Includes bibliographical references and index.
  ISBN 1-56847-176-9
  1. Materials—Juvenile literature. [1. Materials.] I. Title. II. Title:
Material resources. III. Series.
TA403.2.K43   1994
670—dc20   94-8676

Printed in Italy

Other books in the series
Energy Resources
Food Resources
Mineral Resources

Cover pictures (top to bottom): Sisal factory, glass fibers, sheet metal pressing, map of Canadian forest products; (cutout) hot-air balloon.

The Maps
This book contains two kinds of map: world maps, like the one below and area maps, which show only parts of the world. The map below will help you to locate the regions shown in the area maps. Each of the red boxes on this map outlines one of the regions shown in the book. Each box also contains the number of the page on which you can find detailed information about that region.

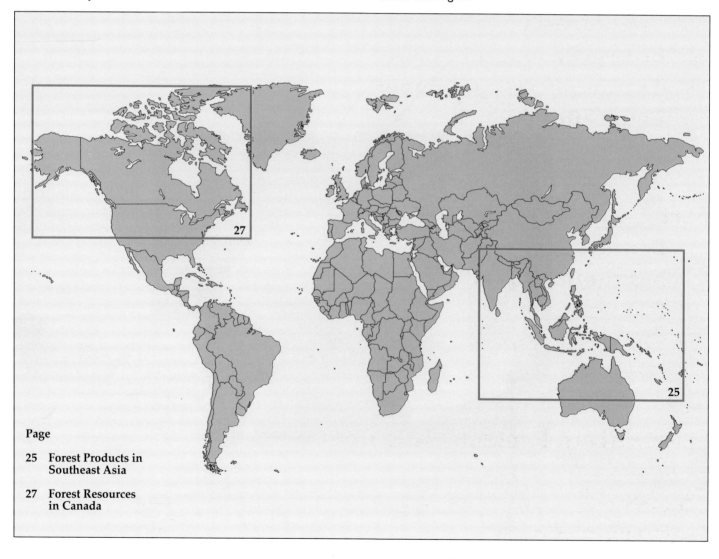

Page

CONTENTS

Introduction

Look around you. How many different kinds of materials can you see? The chances are that you will see a number of metals, several kinds of plastics, products made from wood (including the paper of this book) and other plant fibers, and maybe animal fibers (such as your clothes), glass, and concrete.

Metals, plastics, wood, fibers, glass, and concrete are among the most common materials used to make the thousands of different products we come across in our everyday lives. Of these, the most important by far are the metals.

Can you imagine what life would be like without metals? We would still be living in a stone, bone, and wood age. In particular, without metals, we would not be able to build machines, and machines are vital in all branches of life – in industry, transportation, and business, as well as in the home.

The early periods in the history of civilization are described broadly by the metals that were used, such as Bronze Age (beginning in about 3000 B.C.) and Iron Age (from about 1200 B.C.). It was the widespread use of bronze and, later, iron that helped civilization to advance so rapidly. Since the middle of the 19th century we have lived in what can be called a Steel Age. Today the world uses more than seven hundred billion tons of steel every year. This is nearly 40 times the amount of aluminum used, which is the next most important metal in the modern world.

We could also say that we live in a Plastics Age, because plastics are nearly as important as metals in our world. For many common uses, plastics have replaced traditional materials such as wood, plant and animal fibers, glass, and pottery.

▶ The strength of steel allows architects to design buildings such as the Lloyd's of London office. This building could not have been built without steel.

PART ONE

Metals

In our everyday lives we use only about 20 metals in reasonably large quantities. Iron, aluminum, and copper are by far the most important.

Iron, in the form of steel, is the main structural metal. It is used to make engines and all kinds of other machines, car bodies, bicycle frames, and so on. Steel rods and girders provide the skeleton for the tallest bridges and skyscrapers. Steel is used because it is strong and can be produced in plentiful supply.

Aluminum is both light and strong and is the main metal used for building aircraft. Copper is most widely used in the form of wire in electrical equipment, because it conducts (passes on) electricity with little resistance.

Some metals can be stretched readily without breaking. A metal with this property is called ductile. Copper is very ductile, which allows it to be drawn into fine wire, and this increases its usefulness as a conductor of electricity.

▼ Engineers use steel to build large-scale structures, such as the bridge across Sydney Harbor in Australia.

The World's Major Iron and Copper Resources

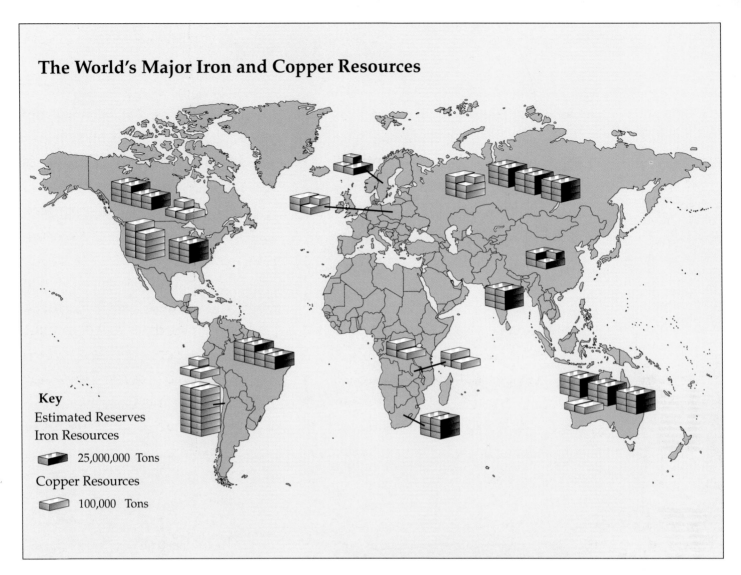

Key
Estimated Reserves
Iron Resources
25,000,000 Tons

Copper Resources
100,000 Tons

Copper has the advantage over steel that it is not very reactive – which means it does not easily react, or combine, with other chemicals. Thus, it does not combine with chemicals in the air to rust, or corrode, as steel does.

Very reactive metals are not normally used in their pure form. For example, the metal sodium is so reactive that it combines vigorously with water, producing hydrogen, which may burst into flame.

◀ Copper is an excellent conductor of electricity, and so it is used for many electrical products. The coil in this transformer is made of copper wire.

Alloys

Steel is not a pure metal. It is mainly iron, but it also contains tiny amounts of other metals, as well as the nonmetal carbon. We call it an alloy of iron. An alloy is either a mixture of metals or a mixture of metals and nonmetals.

Most metals are used in the form of alloys rather than in their pure state. This is because in general pure metals are relatively weak, but they become much stronger when other metals or nonmetals are mixed with them. For example, copper and zinc are soft, weak metals. But if they are mixed together, the result is the alloy called brass, which is hard and strong.

Another reason for mixing different metals together is to produce an alloy with better properties. Ordinary steel rusts, but if you add small amounts of chromium and nickel to it, it becomes stainless steel, which does not rust.

Adding chromium and tungsten to steel produces an alloy with the strength of steel, the hardness of chromium, and the heat resistance of tungsten, which is the metal with the highest melting point (6,000 °F). The result is tungsten steel, a metal used to make cutting tools that stay hard and sharp even when they become red-hot.

Copper is widely used in alloys. Mixed with tin, it forms the alloy bronze, which is used to make some coins and is a favorite material for casting statues. Bronze was the first metal used on a large scale throughout the world.

Mixed with nickel, copper forms the alloy cupronickel. This is used to make silver-colored coins. Mixed with nickel and zinc, copper forms nickel silver, also called German silver. This is used for making ornaments and is the main metal in plated silverware. Cutlery marked with the letters

▼ Cornwall, England, is famous for its tin mines, a few of which are still in production, although many have been exhausted.

EPNS is electroplated nickel silver, which means that the nickel silver is coated with a thin layer of silver by means of a special process called electrolysis (see page 14). Copper and aluminum form an alloy called duralumin. This is the main alloy used in aircraft construction.

Other interesting alloys include invar, an iron-nickel alloy. It is remarkable because it hardly expands or contracts at all when the temperature changes. Because of this, it is used in the manufacture of precision instruments that must remain accurate whatever the conditions. Another unusual alloy is osmiridium, which is very hard and is used to tip the nibs of fountain pens. It is a combination of osmium and iridium – two metals similar to platinum. Osmium is the densest substance known: it is twice as dense as lead and more than 22 times as dense as water.

▲ Modern aircraft are built using aluminum alloys, which are both light and strong.

The Composition of an Alloy

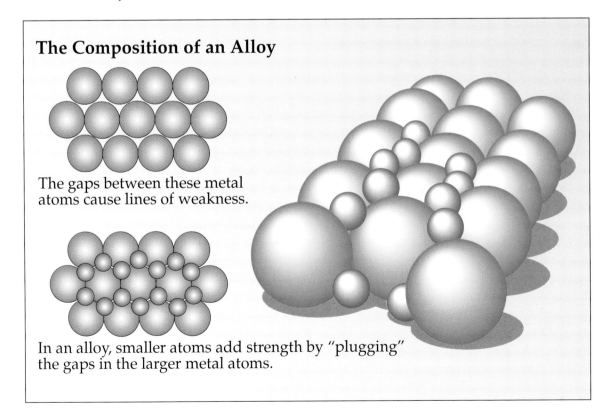

The gaps between these metal atoms cause lines of weakness.

In an alloy, smaller atoms add strength by "plugging" the gaps in the larger metal atoms.

Native Metals

O f all the metals in the earth's crust, only a few are found as pure metal. These native metals include copper, gold, silver, and platinum.

Copper was the first metal to be used widely, more than 5,000 years ago. Gold and silver were also used then in small quantities to make jewelry. Platinum was first produced in commercial quantities, in the 18th century.

Gold and silver

The main use for gold and silver down the ages has been for making jewelry and ornaments. It is easy to understand why. They have an attractive color and shine, and both can be shaped easily into fine jewelry. Exquisite gold jewelry found in Egyptian tombs 5,000 years old is as bright today as when it was made.

Gold does not corrode easily because it is chemically inert – it does not readily combine with other substances. Silver is less inert than gold – for instance, it is slowly tarnished by air, which oxidizes the metal and causes black silver oxide to form on the surface.

Gold and silver are still quite rare. Only about 2,000 tons of gold and 14,000 tons of silver are produced each year. South Africa is the largest producer of gold, while Mexico produces the most silver.

The main use for gold today is for jewelry, although it was once used widely for coinage. It is generally used as an alloy, mixed with silver or copper, which make it harder. Gold is also used in the electronics industry because it is an excellent conductor of electricity and does not corrode easily.

Some silver is used in jewelry and for decorative objects such as

► The death mask of King Tutankhamen of Egypt is made of gold and the blue semiprecious stone called lapis lazuli. The mask was made more than 3,300 years ago.

picture frames, but most is used in photography. Some chemical compounds of silver, such as silver bromide, are sensitive to light and are used to coat photographic film.

Platinum is rarer than gold and silver and is more valuable. Unlike gold and silver, however, it is a hard metal in its pure form. Because of its rarity, malleability, and resistance to corrosion, platinum is also used in jewelry, but it is mainly used in industry as a catalyst in chemical processes such as oil refining. A catalyst is a substance that speeds up chemical processes but is not itself changed.

▲ Many coins were once made of silver.

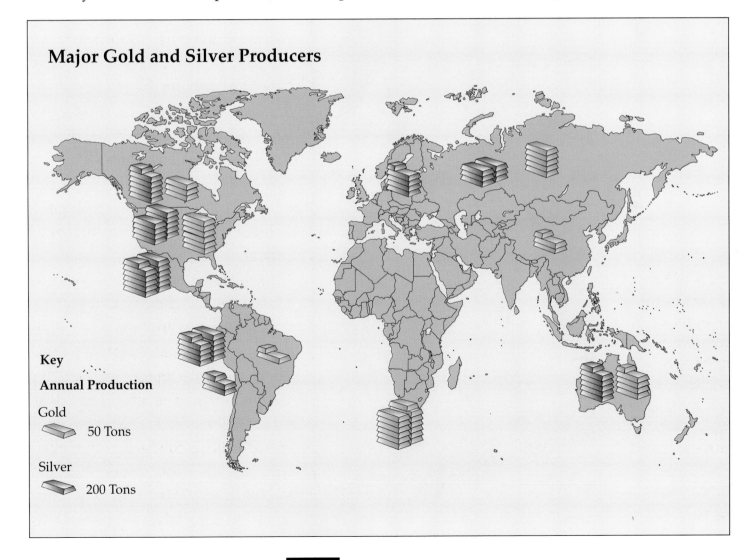

Major Gold and Silver Producers

Key

Annual Production

Gold
50 Tons

Silver
200 Tons

Extracting Metals

▶ Molten copper is formed into specially shaped molds before being refined further by electrolysis.

Most metals are found in the ground in the form of chemical compounds, in which the metal is combined with other elements. These compounds are called mineral ores.

The usual way of extracting a metal from its mineral ore is by a process called smelting. This involves heating the ore in a furnace with other materials to very high temperatures, so that it breaks down, setting the metal free.

Iron, lead, zinc, and copper are metals that are extracted from their ores by smelting.

Some metals are extracted from their ores by electrolysis. In this process electricity is passed through a liquid form of the ore. The electricity splits up the metal compounds so the metal alone can be removed (see page 14).

Aluminum is produced by the electrolysis of its ore when it is in a molten state. Copper can also be extracted from its ore by electrolysis, but the ore must be dissolved first. The ore is treated with acid and the copper dissolves, forming compounds called salts. Then the solution of copper salts is electrolyzed to extract the pure metal.

Iron smelting

Smelting iron ore is one of the most important of all industrial processes. Iron smelting takes place in blast furnaces, so called because hot air is blasted into them to make their fuel burn more fiercely. These furnaces are steel towers up to 180 feet tall, lined with heat-resistant firebrick. Blast furnaces work nonstop for weeks at a time and can produce up to 10,000 tons of iron a day.

Iron ore, limestone, and coke (a fuel with a high carbon content made from coal) are put into the blast furnace. The coke burns fiercely so that temperatures of nearly 3,000 °F can be reached. The coke also reduces the iron ore to metallic iron. Earthy materials and other impurities in the ore combine with the limestone to form a waste product called slag.

◄ Molten copper emerges from the smelting furnace during the refining process.

At the high temperature in the furnace, both the iron and the slag are molten and collect at the bottom of the furnace. From time to time, the furnace is "tapped," and the iron and slag are removed.

The iron produced from a blast furnace is called pig iron. Most of it is processed further to form steel, but some is used directly as cast iron, so called because it is poured or cast into preshaped molds and used in this form.

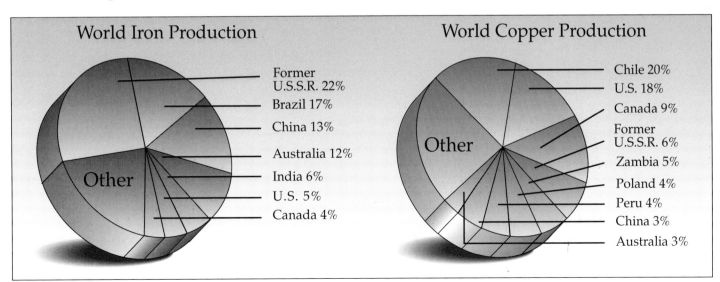

World Iron Production

Former U.S.S.R. 22%
Brazil 17%
China 13%
Australia 12%
India 6%
U.S. 5%
Canada 4%
Other

World Copper Production

Chile 20%
U.S. 18%
Canada 9%
Former U.S.S.R. 6%
Zambia 5%
Poland 4%
Peru 4%
China 3%
Australia 3%
Other

Refining Metals

Metals that have been extracted from their ores by smelting and other methods usually contain some impurities. Normally these have to be removed before the metal can be used. This purifying process is called refining.

Not all impurities are wasted. Sometimes, the impurities are more valuable than the metal being purified. This is the case with some lead, zinc, and nickel ores, which often contain small amounts of gold and silver.

Pig iron has to be refined before it can be turned into steel. This takes place in a furnace. Other metals are refined electrically, by means of electrolysis.

Steelmaking

The Romans knew how to make a kind of steel about 2,000 years ago. But steel was not made on a large scale until 1856, when a British industrialist, Henry Bessemer, developed the first process for producing steel cheaply. In the Bessemer process, air is blasted through the molten pig iron. Impurities in the iron combine with the oxygen in the air and are literally burned out.

REFINING BY ELECTROLYSIS

Several metals are purified by means of electrolysis. Copper, lead, gold, silver, and nickel are among metals refined in this way. The electrolysis of copper is an example. The impure copper is made into plates and placed in a solution of a copper compound (such as copper sulfate), along with plates of pure copper. Electricity is then passed through the solution between the two sets of plates. The impure plates are connected to the positive terminal of the electricity supply, the pure plates to the negative. As electrolysis proceeds, copper is dissolved from the impure plates and is deposited as pure copper on the pure plates (right).

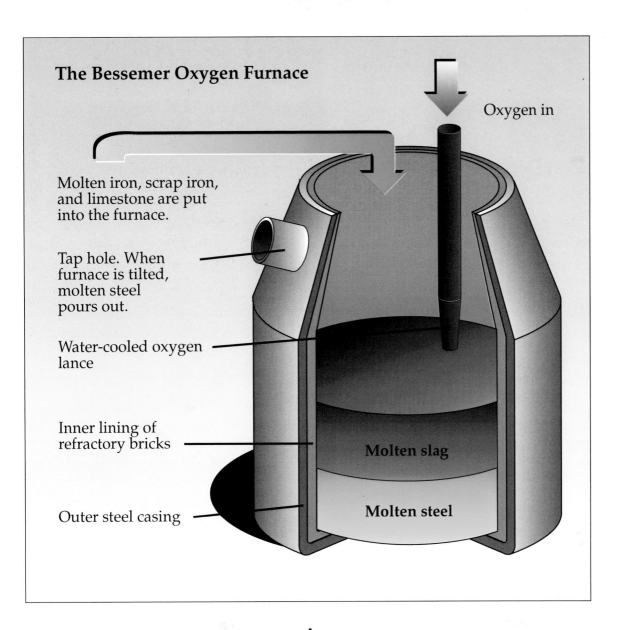

The Bessemer Oxygen Furnace

Oxygen in

Molten iron, scrap iron, and limestone are put into the furnace.

Tap hole. When furnace is tilted, molten steel pours out.

Water-cooled oxygen lance

Inner lining of refractory bricks

Outer steel casing

Molten slag

Molten steel

The commonest method of steelmaking today has developed from the Bessemer process. It is known as the basic oxygen process, which uses pure oxygen rather than air to burn out the impurities in the iron. The finest steels, however, are made in an electric furnace, using steel scrap.

The basic oxygen process takes place in a tiltable furnace called a converter. Molten pig iron is put into the converter, along with steel scrap and limestone. Then a jet of pure oxygen is blasted into the mixture. This burns out most of the carbon in the iron, which is the main impurity. Other impurities combine with the limestone to form a slag. The metallic product is steel, which is removed while it is still molten for further processing.

Shaping Hot Metal

▶ Intricate molds, called dies, are used in a process called die-casting to form metals into complex shapes.

Metals can be shaped in several different ways. A metal can be melted and poured, or cast, into a mold. A hard metal such as iron can be heated until it is red-hot, to soften it, then beaten into a new shape.

A soft metal such as copper or gold can be stretched or beaten when cold.

Casting is one of the simplest and also one of the oldest methods of shaping metal. The workshop where casting takes place is called

▲ Many car engine parts are shaped by casting.

a foundry. A casting is made by pouring molten metal into a mold of the desired shape. When the metal cools, it takes the shape of the mold.

A common cast product is a car engine block, which is made of cast iron. Cast iron is hard and rigid and absorbs shocks well, but it is brittle, so it cannot be used to make things that must be flexible.

The molds used for casting are often made from a special type of sand that binds together well. Permanent metal molds, which are called dies, may also be used. Casting in dies, or die-casting, is now widely used for the mass production of small castings for domestic appliances such as a steam iron or for metal toys.

In the die-casting process, molten metal alloy is injected into water-cooled dies.

Hot but solid metal may be shaped by rolling, forging, or pressing. In rolling, a slab of hot metal is squeezed thinner and thinner as it is passed back and forth between heavy rollers. In forging, hot metal is hammered into shape. This is how blacksmiths shape metal. In industry, massive machines called drop forges do the hammering, forcing the metal into shape in dies. In pressing, powerful presses exerting pressures of thousands of tons squeeze metal into shape.

◄ A blacksmith hammers red-hot iron to beat it into the shape he wants.

Shaping Cold Metal

Several of the methods used to shape cold metal are similar to those used to shape it when it is hot. Sheet metal, for example, is often rolled cold after it has been rolled hot. Cold rolling gives the metal a more accurate finish and also makes it harder. However, shaping a metal when it is cold can make it stiff and brittle, and this can be a disadvantage for some products.

Cold-rolled metal can be made less brittle by a process called annealing, in which it is first heated and then allowed to cool slowly.

Sheet steel is normally pressed into shape when it is cold using powerful presses. This method is used to shape the body panels for cars, for example.

Metals are drawn out into wire when they are cold. In drawing, a metal rod is pulled through a series of dies, each slightly smaller than the one before, so the metal is squeezed and stretched.

Cold metal is also hammered into shape in dies. This method is used in the production of coins, for example. The process is called stamping.

MACHINING

After a piece of metal has been shaped by casting, forging, pressing, or another process, it usually still requires further attention to bring it to its final form. Most finishing processes involve cutting or grinding away some of the metal. This operation is carried out by machines called machine tools and is called machining. There are many types of machine tools, which are all driven by powerful motors. The most common machine tool is the lathe (left), which cuts by a process called turning. The power drill bores into metal with a rotating bit. Milling machines cut metal with rotating toothed wheels. Grinding machines remove metal with a rotating wheel made of rough abrasive.

Major Crude Steel Producers

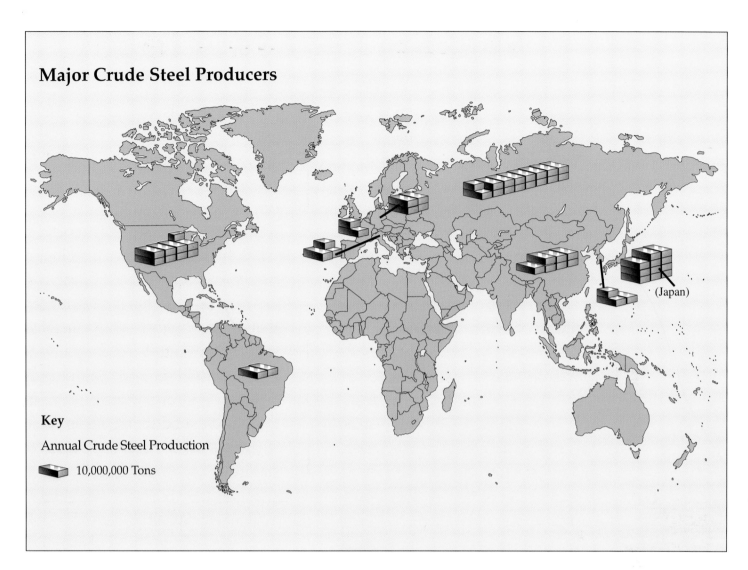

Key

Annual Crude Steel Production

10,000,000 Tons

(Japan)

▶ Cold sheet metal can be pressed into a new shape in a heavy press. This sheet is being fed into the press before shaping.

Jewelers and metal craft workers may shape metals such as gold or copper by hammering it gently. A strong yet flexible metal such as gold can be hammered into a sheet so thin that it becomes almost transparent. In this form it is known as gold leaf.

PART TWO

Wood and Natural Fibers

Wood was one of the first materials human beings used on a large scale, and huge amounts of wood are still used throughout the world. Wood is used in the construction industry, to build houses and to make furniture, for example. Much is converted into pulp products, such as paper. But by far the biggest use of wood is as firewood for cooking and heating.

Thick forests once covered most of the land areas of the earth, where the soil and climate were suitable. But as civilizations developed, farmers cut down forests to get more land for grazing animals and growing crops. Even though few forests remain, those that survive are still being cut down to provide extra farmland or lumber. In many tropical countries the destruction of the forests is happening on such a large scale that it is devastating the environment.

Fibers from plants and animals have provided the basic materials for making clothing and other textiles for at least 5,000 years. Natural fibers are first gathered together and drawn out into long threads, in a process called spinning. Then sets of threads can be interlaced to produce cloth, in a process called weaving.

Cotton from plants and wool from sheep or other animals are the main natural fibers that are spun and woven into cloth. But these and other natural fibers are being replaced in many textiles by manufactured fibers, such as rayon, nylon, polyesters, and acrylics. Rayon is made from wood pulp, while other manufactured fibers are made from different kinds of plastics that can be drawn out into long threads.

▶ Indians in Guatemala still use traditional spinning and weaving techniques to make fabrics.

◀ Wood has been used as a building material since earliest times. It is still used today where supplies are plentiful, to build homes such as this log cabin in Yukon Territory, Canada.

The Forests

The biggest stretches of forest remaining in the world extend in a broad belt across the north of North America, Europe, and Asia. Taken together they are called the boreal (northern) forest, and they cover much of Alaska and Canada, Scandinavia, and Russia (where the forest is called the taiga). In places the forest reaches inside the Arctic Circle.

The typical tree of the boreal forest is the conifer. This tree has tiny, needlelike leaves and bears its seeds in cones. Spruce, fir, and pine are common conifers. They are evergreens, keeping their leaves all year long. They are also known as softwoods because of the relatively soft texture of their wood, which is used for some building purposes and to make pulp for paper.

Deciduous forests

South of the boreal forest in North America, Europe, and Asia, the native forests have all but disappeared. This is where most of the population live. The scattered natural forests that survive are made up mainly of deciduous trees with broad leaves.

Deciduous trees are those that shed their leaves in autumn. They include oak, ash, birch, chestnut, elm, maple, and poplar. The wood from some of these trees, such as oak, is hard and durable, and has been used for centuries for building houses and furniture, as well as wooden ships.

Tropical rain forests

These forests grow in tropical countries around the equator, where it is hot and there is plenty of rain all year long. In this hot, moist climate, trees and other vegetation grow very quickly. The typical trees of rain forests have broad leaves and are evergreen.

▼ Peyto Lake, in Alberta, Canada, is surrounded by forests of conifer trees.

▶ The Ucayali river winds through the dense rain forest in Amazonia.

They grow, flower, and fruit throughout the year. Among the best-known species are mahogany, teak and ebony. These trees produce some of the hardest woods, which are valued highly for making and decorating houses and furniture. The demand for these hardwoods is one of the main causes of the destruction of rain forests in Southeast Asia in particular.

World Forests

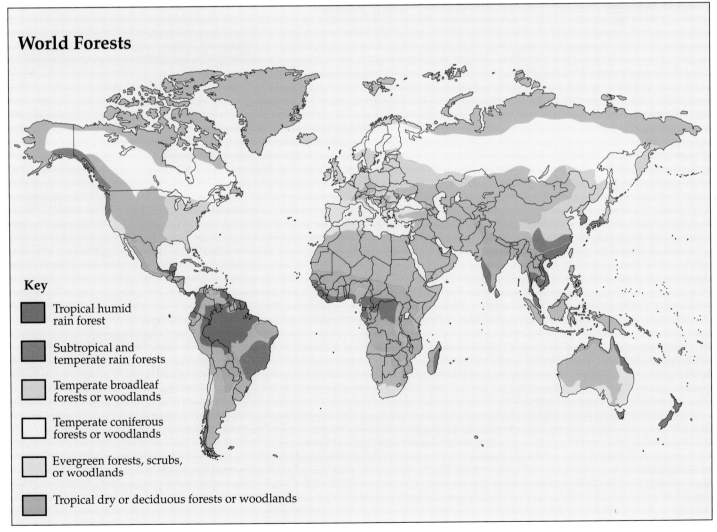

Key

■ Tropical humid rain forest

■ Subtropical and temperate rain forests

□ Temperate broadleaf forests or woodlands

□ Temperate coniferous forests or woodlands

□ Evergreen forests, scrubs, or woodlands

■ Tropical dry or deciduous forests or woodlands

Forest Products

The main product of most forests is the wood of the trees. The trees are felled (cut down) and transported to sawmills or pulp mills.

Apart from wood, forest products include turpentine, which is extracted from the sap of pine trees, and rubber, made from the sap of rubber trees.

In many countries, natural forests are felled with little concern for the future. But in some countries, new forests are being planted to replace those that are being cut down. In such cases, the trees are being farmed as a crop, rather than mined like a mineral.

The most widely planted trees are quick-growing conifers, but these are in general suitable only for cooler climates. They are no substitute for the slow-growing hardwoods being felled elsewhere.

Foresters may rely on existing trees to reseed a felled area, or they may plant seedlings they have raised in a nursery. As with other cultivated crops, the growing trees must be tended until they have become established, in order to protect them from pests and diseases.

RAISING RUBBER

Rubber is obtained from the rubber tree, *Hevea brasiliensis*, which is native to the Amazon region of South America. But most rubber is now produced by large plantations in Malaysia, Indonesia, and Thailand. The trees in these plantations are descendants of seedlings of the wild rubber tree brought into the region in the 1870s. The rubber tree, which grows to about 45-60 feet tall, is harvested by tapping. The tapper makes a sloping cut in the bark and attaches a small spout and a cup at the lower end. Sap, or latex, oozes out and drips into the cup. The tapper returns a few hours later to collect it (above). The latex is later treated with acid to make it coagulate, or become solid. This gives crude rubber, which is then sent for further processing.

Logging

The process of felling trees and removing them from the forest is called logging. Trees are usually cut down with a motor-driven chain saw. Trees that have been growing for 150 years or more, weighing 50 tons and standing 50 feet tall, can be cut down using a powerful chain saw in just a few minutes.

Methods of taking felled timber out of the forest vary from place to place. In some forests in southern Asia, elephants are used. But elsewhere, massive tractors are used, and these cause great damage to the forest environment.

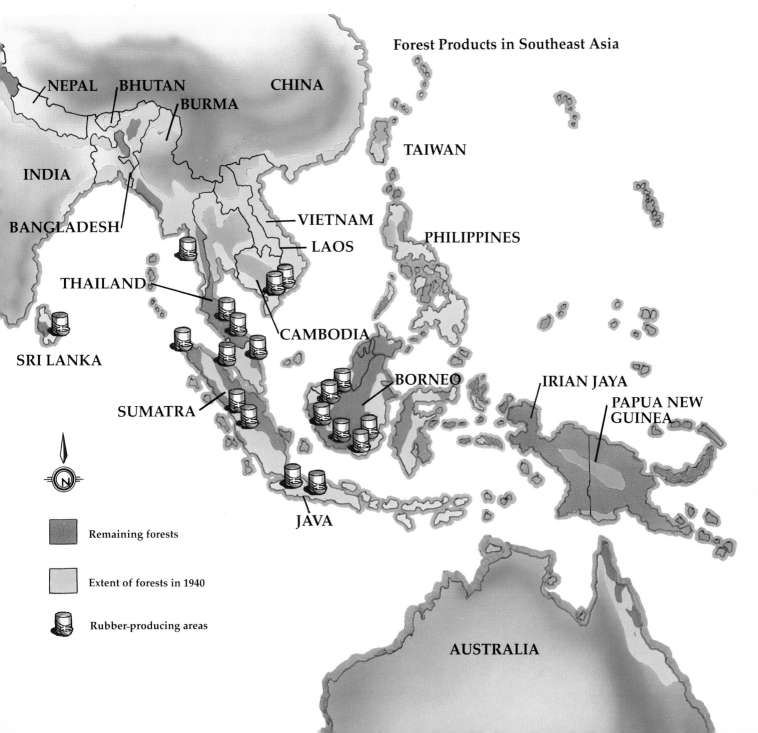

Forest Products in Southeast Asia

NEPAL BHUTAN CHINA
BURMA
INDIA
TAIWAN
BANGLADESH
VIETNAM
LAOS
PHILIPPINES
THAILAND
CAMBODIA
SRI LANKA
BORNEO IRIAN JAYA
SUMATRA PAPUA NEW GUINEA
JAVA
AUSTRALIA

Remaining forests

Extent of forests in 1940

Rubber-producing areas

Timber, Pulp, and Paper

After logs have been taken out of the forest, they are transported to the saw-mill or pulp mill by road, rail, river, or canal.

In the sawmill, the logs are fed by conveyer to band or frame saws, which slice them into boards. Other saws trim and cut them to size. Afterward, the sawn wood is stacked and left to dry out. This seasoning process can take from a few days to a year, depending on the type of wood.

The building industry uses vast amounts of sawn timber, or lumber. Mostly, it is the relatively soft wood from conifer trees.

Softwood lumber is used in buildings for floor and ceiling joists, in the roof, and for door and window frames. Flooring is often made from wooden boards or from plywood, which is made of thin layers of wood glued together.

Lumber from deciduous trees, such as oak, and tropical trees, such as mahogany, is much harder and is called hardwood. It is often used for making furniture and sometimes is applied as a thin slice, or veneer, to a cheaper softwood.

Making pulp and paper

Softwood timber is the main raw material for making wood pulp, from which paper and other products are made. The amount of wood needed every year just to make paper is enormous. It is equivalent to an area of forest the size of Sweden.

In the pulp mill, the logs first have their bark removed. Then they are made into pulp by either a mechanical or chemical process. In the mechanical process, the logs are shredded into fibers by a set of revolving grinders. In the chemical process, they are cooked with chemicals. This treatment reduces

▼ A sawmill, such as this one in Manjimup, Western Australia, processes logs into sawn timber.

the wood to fibers. The resulting mass of fibers is known as wood pulp.

The pulp is dried into sheets and transported to the paper factory. There it is mixed with water and substances such as clay and resin before passing to the papermaking machine. The mixture flows onto a moving wire-mesh belt, and the water drains away. The wet web that results is dried and rolled and emerges as paper sheet.

How Paper Is Made

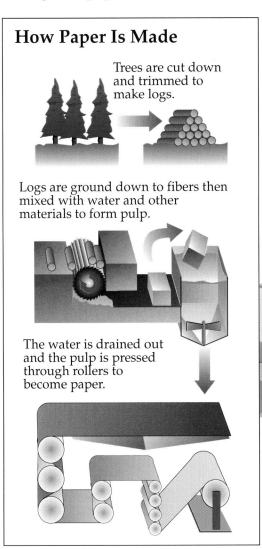

Trees are cut down and trimmed to make logs.

Logs are ground down to fibers then mixed with water and other materials to form pulp.

The water is drained out and the pulp is pressed through rollers to become paper.

Key   **Forest Resources in Canada**

- Tundra
- **Boreal Forest**
- **Temperate Deciduous Forest**
- **Mountain Vegetation**
- **Humid Grassland**
- **Warm Temperate Forest**
- **Desert Scrub**
- **Paper Pulp Production**
- **Timber Production**

▲ Paper for newsprint is delivered in huge rolls, looking like the tree trunks from which the paper was originally made.

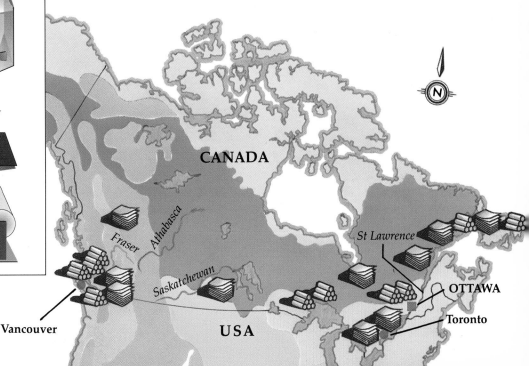

Plant Fibers

The first plant fiber used for spinning and weaving into cloth was cotton. Cultivation of cotton for this purpose began about 5,000 years ago, in the Indus Valley in Pakistan, and cotton is still the natural fiber that is most widely used today.

Cotton plants grow only in tropical and subtropical regions. China produces the most cotton, and India, Pakistan, and the United States (in its southern states) are also major producers. The world production of cotton is approximately 12 million tons a year.

The cotton plant is a small shrub. The fibers grow inside the seed bolls (pods). When ripe, the bolls burst open to expose a fluffy mass of fine fibers. In poorer countries the cotton is still picked by hand, but in the United States huge mechanical cotton pickers do the work.

After picking, the long cotton fibers, called lint, are separated from the seeds by a cotton gin. The shorter fibers, called linters, are not good for spinning, but they are a valuable raw material because they are pure cellulose. They can be made into cellulose plastics, such as celluloid, and artificial fibers, such as rayon and acetate.

Fibers that are as smooth as silk, but much less expensive, can be produced artificially by processing cotton. Viscose rayon is the one produced in the largest quantities.

To make viscose rayon, a mass of cotton linters is treated with chemicals until it forms a syrupy solution. This solution is then pumped through the tiny holes of a spinneret into an acid bath. The acid changes the fine streams of viscose liquid into threads of pure cellulose. Finally, the threads are gathered and twisted together to make rayon yarn.

▼ A sisal factory in João Pessoa, Brazil. Sisal is a ropy fiber produced from the leaves of agave plants.

Major Natural Fiber Producers

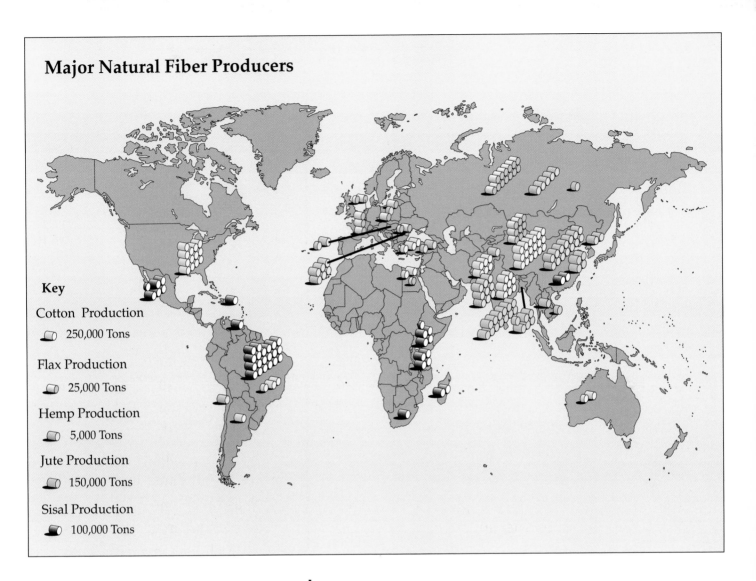

Key

Cotton Production
🗞 250,000 Tons

Flax Production
🗞 25,000 Tons

Hemp Production
🗞 5,000 Tons

Jute Production
🗞 150,000 Tons

Sisal Production
🗞 100,000 Tons

Other commercial fiber crops include flax, jute, and sisal.

Flax is the most important fiber crop after cotton, because it is the plant from which linen fibers are obtained. It grows best in the cool climate of northern Europe. The fibers are taken from the stalks of the plant, which is cultivated like wheat. The plant is also grown for its seeds, which yield linseed oil.

Jute is extracted from the stalks of jute plants. These plants, which grow on average to a height of about 12 feet, are widely cultivated in India and Pakistan. Jute is a coarse, tough fiber, used to make sacking and ropes.

Sisal is a strong fiber obtained from the swordlike leaves of the tropical agave plants sisalana and henequen, after the fleshy pulp is removed. It is used for making ropes and binding twine. Brazil, Mexico, and Tanzania are leading producers of sisal.

Animal Fibers

The wool from the curly fleece of sheep is the most widely used animal fiber, although goats and camels also produce fibers. The most prized animal fiber is silk, taken from the cocoon spun by the silkworm.

Most wool comes from merino breeds of sheep. They produce heavy fleeces, up to 26 pounds per sheep. About 1.7 million tons of wool are produced in the world every year. Australia is the biggest producer and has the most sheep: approximately 165 million, which is more than ten times its human population.

MAKING SILK

The Chinese discovered the secret of making silk nearly 5,000 years ago, and they are still one of the world's leading producers. Silk is produced in a cocoon as part of the life cycle of a large cream-colored moth, with the scientific name of *Bombyx mori*.

The cycle begins when the moth lays its eggs on the leaves of mulberry trees. The eggs hatch into tiny larvae, known as silkworms. The silkworms eat the mulberry leaves and grow rapidly.

After about five weeks, when they are fully grown, each silkworm starts to spin a cocoon of very fine thread around itself. The thread is produced from a spinning gland called a spinneret in a continuous length of more than 2,000 feet. When the cocoon is complete, the farmers kill the silkworms and carefully unravel the long thin threads from the cocoons (above). Several threads may be twisted together to make strong yarn.

▼ Wool is cut from sheep by sheepshearers, using large electric clippers.

The long hair from angora and cashmere goats makes excellent textile fibers. The hair from the angora breed is known as mohair. Angora goats came originally from Turkey, but they are now also farmed on a large scale in Texas, South America, and South Africa. They are sheared for their fleece, just like sheep.

The cashmere goat, originally from Tibet and northern India, provides a very soft fiber called cashmere. This fiber is the soft, downy fur that grows under the goat's coarse outer coat. It is combed out when the animal molts.

The softest fibers of all come from the coat of the vicuña. This animal belongs to the camel family and lives in the Andes Mountains in South America at heights above 10,000 feet. The fibers of its inner fleece are less than half as thick as the finest sheep's wool.

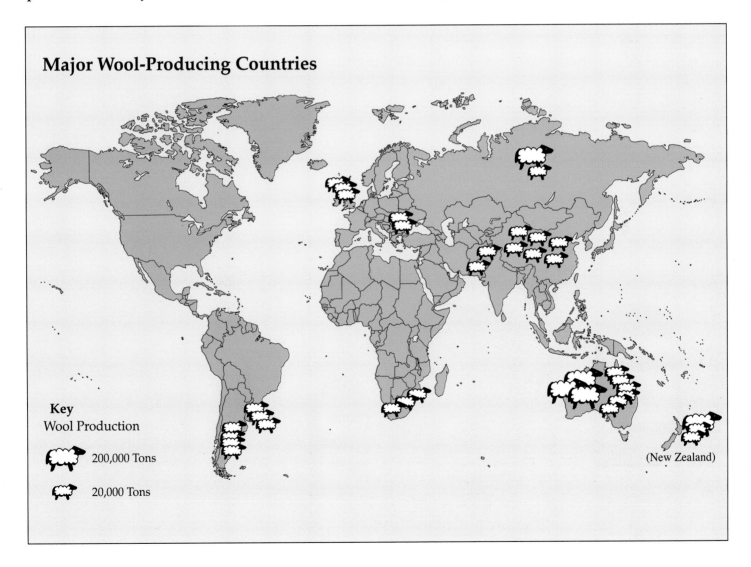

Major Wool-Producing Countries

Key
Wool Production

200,000 Tons

20,000 Tons

(New Zealand)

Manufactured Materials

▼ Petroleum can be broken down, in a process called cracking, so that large molecules form different smaller ones. Then further treatment, called polymerization, using high temperature and pressure, can convert some of these small molecules into plastics.

Many materials in use today are totally different from the raw materials from which they are made. Pottery is made from clay, which is powdery when dry. Glass is made from sand and limestone. And many kinds of plastics are made from oil.

Of all such manufactured materials, plastics are the most important in the modern world. They have replaced traditional materials such as wood, resins, fibers, pottery, and even metal for many uses.

Plastics are synthetic materials, made from chemicals, mostly obtained from crude oil, or petroleum. Over 50 million tons of plastics are produced every year.

A useful characteristic of many manufactured materials is that they can be shaped easily. Pottery is shaped from wet clay by a potter's hands. Glass may be shaped by a glassblower who blows the molten glass into its desired shape. Pottery and glass can also be shaped in a mold. Pottery is hardened by baking, and molten glass hardens as it grows cold.

Plastics are very easily shaped by molding, which makes it possible to manufacture products from them cheaply. Also, they are waterproof and easy to wipe clean, and many plastics are also flexible. This flexibility makes plastics less breakable than pottery or glass.

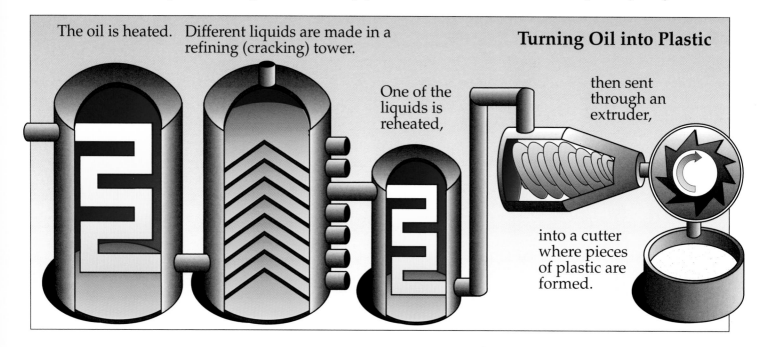

The oil is heated. Different liquids are made in a refining (cracking) tower.

Turning Oil into Plastic

One of the liquids is reheated,

then sent through an extruder,

into a cutter where pieces of plastic are formed.

Plastics have these properties because their basic particles, or molecules, are made up of long, flexible chains of carbon atoms. Most other materials have short molecules, which do not hold together as well.

One of today's best-known plastics is polyethylene used, for example, for making basins and transparent bags. Other common plastics are PVC (polyvinyl chloride), used for kitchen flooring, pipes, and imitation leather; polystyrene, used for kitchen containers and as a foam for packaging; and Lucite, used instead of glass for windshields, serving pieces, and watch crystals.

Many plastics soften when they are reheated. They are known as thermoplastics. But others, called thermosets, are hard and do not soften when they are reheated. The original synthetic plastic, Bakelite, was a thermoset, first made by the Belgian chemist Leo Baekeland in 1907. It is still used today because it is heat-resistant and is an excellent electrical insulator. One of the newest thermosets is superglue, which sets instantly when applied.

▶ Plastic is the best material to use for making light, bright, washable toys such as plastic masks.

Plastics

▼ Plastics can be formed into all kinds of shapes, such as these old-style and new-style telephones.

One of the biggest advantages of plastics over many other materials is the ease with which they can be shaped. In particular, this makes them suitable for manufacture by mass-production methods.

The commonest way of shaping plastics is by molding. There are three main molding methods: blow molding, injection molding, and compression molding. The first two are commonly used with thermoplastics. Compression molding is used to shape thermosets.

Molding methods

Blow molding is used to make hollow objects, such as bottles. A tube of hot, soft plastic is inserted into a cooled mold and then air is blown into it. The plastic is forced against the walls of the mold and takes their shape as it cools.

Injection molding is used to make toys and bowls. The plastic is heated and then forced into a cooled mold, where it cools and sets hard.

Thermosets cannot be shaped like thermoplastics because they set as they are heated. So they are shaped using a molding resin, which is a halfway stage to the plastic. The resin is placed in the bottom half of a heated mold, then the top half is immediately pressed down on it. The resin is shaped as it sets.

Blown Plastic Molding

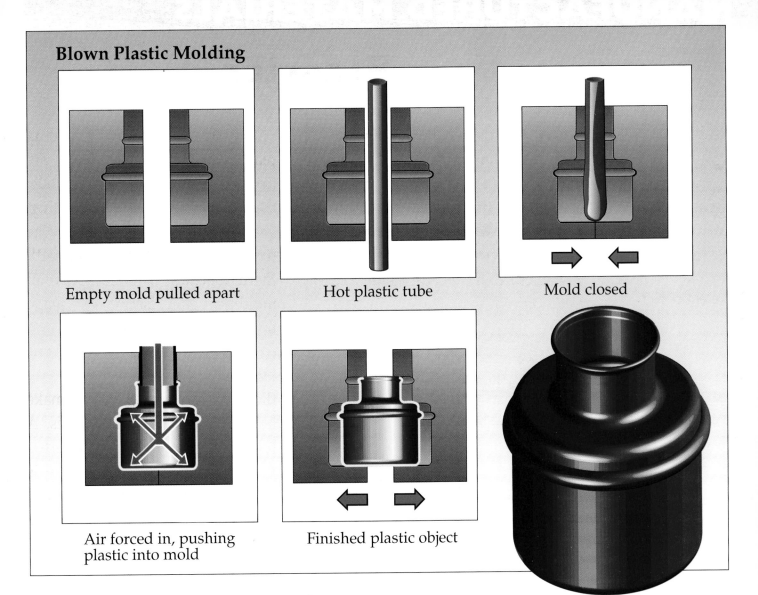

Empty mold pulled apart

Hot plastic tube

Mold closed

Air forced in, pushing plastic into mold

Finished plastic object

Other shaping methods

Plastics can also be shaped by a variety of other methods. One method is extrusion, a process in which molten plastic is forced through a die (shaped hole). This method is used to make plastic tubing, by extruding the plastic through a ring-shaped hole.

Laminating is a process in which several layers of materials, soaked in a solution of thermosetting resin, are pressed together and heated. They set to form a solid laminate, which is both durable and heat-resistant. Kitchen countertops are usually made of plastic laminates.

Vacuum-forming is another shaping technique, used to make egg cartons, for example. A plastic sheet is placed over a mold and heated. Then a vacuum is applied so that pressure forces the soft plastic against the inside of the mold, where it sets into shape.

Synthetic Fibers

Some plastic materials can be drawn out when soft into very fine threads, or fibers. Such synthetic fibers are now used on a vast scale by the textile industry, where they have replaced natural fibers for many uses.

An American chemist named Wallace Carothers led a research team that produced the first synthetic fiber in 1935. This fiber, nylon, is still widely used. It has an appearance and feel similar to silk, and is used for making stockings, blouses, shirts, and underwear.

Nylon has been joined by many other synthetic fibers. They include polyester and acrylic fibers. All are made from petrochemicals.

Synthetic fibers have several advantages over natural fibers. They are much stronger; they are resistant to attack by moths and other insects; and they do not rot. Also, they do not absorb water, so that they drip dry, and they tend to be crease-resistant.

Spinning the fibers

Synthetic fibers are produced by methods of spinning that imitate the way silkworms spin the threads of their cocoons.

Nylon and polyester fibers are produced by melt spinning. Plastic chips are heated until they melt. Then the molten plastic is pumped into a perforated device called a spinneret and forced out through tiny holes. The thin streams of plastic coming through the holes harden in the air, forming fine fibers.

Another type of synthetic fiber, called acrylic, breaks down when heated, so acrylic fibers are produced by dry or wet spinning. The acrylic plastic is first dissolved in a solvent. In dry spinning, this solution is then pumped through a spinneret into warm air. The solvent evaporates, leaving acrylic fibers. In wet spinning, the streams of solution leaving the spinneret enter a chemical bath, where they change into fibers.

All three methods of spinning produce long threads, or filaments. The filaments may be used as they are to make textiles or they may be chopped into short fibers. These fibers may then be mixed with natural fibers and spun into yarn by normal spinning methods. Most clothing now contains a blend of natural and synthetic fibers.

▶ Hot-air balloons are made of very strong, tear-resistant and heat-resistant synthetic fabrics.

Pottery

Long before humans discovered how to smelt metals, they made objects out of clay soils. They would moisten the clay, shape it, and then bake it in a fire. The result was pottery. Objects made by baking clay, such as pottery or bricks, are called ceramics.

The earliest examples of pottery have been found in the Middle East. Some pieces date back about 9,000 years. This pottery was made wholly by hand. About 5,500 years ago, the potter's wheel came into use, providing a means of turning a lump of clay while the potter shaped it with both hands. This technique is still the main pottery-shaping process used today.

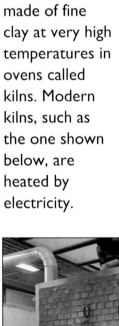

▼ Porcelain is made by baking (firing) objects made of fine clay at very high temperatures in ovens called kilns. Modern kilns, such as the one shown below, are heated by electricity.

▲ A potter in India uses the traditional spinning wheel to help shape the clay.

Three types of pottery

The commonest type of pottery is earthenware. It can be made from a variety of clays and is baked, or fired, in a special kind of oven, called a kiln, at a temperature of about 1,800 °F. Earthenware is not very hard and is also porous, which means water can pass through it. For this reason, it has to be coated, usually with a glassy, waterproof material called a glaze, before it can be used.

A second type of pottery, stoneware, uses finer clays and is

◄ China clay, or kaolin, used to make porcelain, is mined in various parts of the world, including Dartmoor, England.

fired at temperatures greater than 2,200°F. At this temperature, the structure of the clay changes and begins to resemble stone. Stoneware is hard and strong and is not porous. Sewage and drainage pipes are typical stoneware products.

The finest pottery is the third type, porcelain. Its main ingredient is a pure white mineral called kaolin or china clay. The mixture has to be fired at temperatures up to 2,550°F. At such temperatures the pottery becomes extremely hard, but also brittle. Porcelain is used for the most delicate and valuable items of tableware.

Decoration

Potters have decorated their wares from earliest times. They may scratch designs in the clay or paint it. Painting may be done on the clay itself before it has been glazed, or it may be done afterward. In commercial potteries, designs are applied to the pots by mass-produced prints called transfers.

◄ The final porcelain product can be decorated with beautiful designs.

Other Ceramics

Many other kinds of materials are produced by baking earthy ingredients. In general they are called ceramics. They vary from the ordinary bricks used for building houses to the tiles that cover the body of the space shuttle.

Bricks are made from various clays, which are mixed with water and kneaded into a doughy mass. The clay is then extruded, or forced through a rectangular hole to form a rectangular ribbon, which is then cut into brick shapes. In an alternative process, the clay is forced into brick-shaped molds. After shaping, the bricks are fired at a temperature of about 1,800 °F in a kiln, or oven.

▲ Ceramics, which are easily cleaned, can be used to make wall tiles, sinks, and baths – as seen in this modern bathroom.

▶ The special ceramics used to make tiles on the nose and underside of the space shuttle resist the searing heat produced when the craft reenters the atmosphere.

Other kinds of bricks, called fire-bricks, are used to line industrial furnaces. They are made from materials that resist high temperatures, such as silica and alumina.

The general name for a heat-resistant material used in chemical processes is a *refractory* material. One very useful refractory material is graphite, a natural form of carbon. It is used to make crucibles, or pots for holding molten metals and other very hot substances.

Carbon refractory materials are also used on the wings and tail of the space shuttle. When the shuttle returns to earth, friction with the air heats parts of the wings and the tail to temperatures up to 2,700 °F. Other parts of the shuttle are covered with tiles made from silica fibers. These have excellent heat resistance, too.

Silica, the mineral that makes up sand, is also the raw material from which silicon crystal is made. This is the starting point for the manufacture of silicon chips, the tiny wafers that have made possible the present revolution in computing and electronics.

▶ St. Pancras train station in London, England. Finished in 1873, it shows how brickwork can be used to make a building attractive.

Glass

▼ Glass fibers, shown here in an electron microscope photograph, can be woven into sheets to reinforce plastics, forming fiberglass.

Glass is produced from very common ingredients, sand and limestone, two of the most plentiful minerals on earth. Like clay, it is an ancient material, in use in the Middle East at least 5,000 years ago.

Glass is an unusual substance. It is hard, it can be shaped easily, it does not rot, and it is not affected by any common chemical. Very

▲ Fine quality glass, with a high lead content, can be cut and polished precisely. It is called crystal glass.

few substances – one is hydrofluoric acid – attack glass.

Several different kinds of glass are made. Ordinary window glass, known as soda-lime glass, is made from a mixture of pure sand, sodium carbonate, and limestone. These ingredients are heated in a furnace at a temperature of at least 2,700 °F. They melt together to form a liquid that turns into transparent glass when it cools.

Special glasses are made by varying the glassmaking recipe. Adding lead oxide produces crystal glass, noted for its sparkle.

Adding boron oxide and silica produces borosilicate glass, which is useful because it hardly expands when heated or cooled. This makes it suitable for heat-proof containers such as kitchen bowls (Pyrex).

Shaping glass

Glass may be shaped in a variety of ways. Hollow objects, such as bottles and jars, are produced by blowing. Fine glassware is blown by mouth by skilled craftspeople. They dip their blowpipe into molten glass so that a gob (lump) of glass becomes attached. Then they blow into the gob to shape it, adding to it or trimming it until the desired shape is achieved.

Most glassblowing is now done by machine. Air is blown into a gob of glass inside a mold, so that the glass is pressed against the walls and takes the mold's shape.

Flat glass is now made mainly by the float-glass process. A thin layer of molten glass from the furnace flows onto a bath of molten tin, where it slowly cools and becomes solid. Because the surface of the tin is perfectly flat, the glass becomes perfectly flat, too.

For some purposes glass is made in the form of fine fibers. These are produced when molten glass forms delicate filaments as it emerges from fine holes in the bottom of a furnace. Glass fibers are now widely used to reinforce (strengthen) plastics. The resulting material, often just called fiberglass, is properly termed glass-reinforced plastic (GRP). Fluffy glass wool, consisting of a mass of short glass fibers, is widely used for insulating houses.

▲ Red hot, molten glass is blown and molded into shape by skilled craftsmen.

Problems and Prospects

Metals, in the form of mineral ores, are being taken from the earth in huge quantities. Sooner or later, supplies will begin to run out.

Fortunately, two of the world's main metals, iron and aluminum, are plentiful and will last for several hundred years. But many vital metals could start to run out early next century. They include gold, silver, copper, tin, lead, zinc, mercury, tungsten, and platinum.

We should be able to find substitutes for many of these metals, but some will be difficult to replace. Photography, for instance, relies on the light sensitivity of salts of silver – no other metal will do. And no other metal is as good a catalyst as platinum.

▼ Aluminum is used to make cans for drinks. After use, these can be recycled to reclaim the aluminum.

Plastics will play an increasing role as metal substitutes in the form of composites, or mixtures with fibers. Some aircraft are already being built of composites. But plastics depend on chemicals from petroleum, which could also run out next century.

Recycling, or reusing materials, will also help to conserve supplies. The photographic industry already recovers large amounts of silver during the processing of film. Steel, aluminum, and glass manufacturers use large amounts of scrap in production. This also helps conserve another precious commodity: energy. For example, extracting pure aluminum from scrap requires less than one-twentieth of the energy needed to extract it from its ore.

Timber tomorrow

Many of the world's tropical rain forests are being cut down and cleared very rapidly. The most valuable hardwood trees are used, but most trees are simply burned to make way for cattle grazing or crop farming on the cleared land.

If the forests are destroyed, many thousands of species of

The Destruction of the Rain Forests

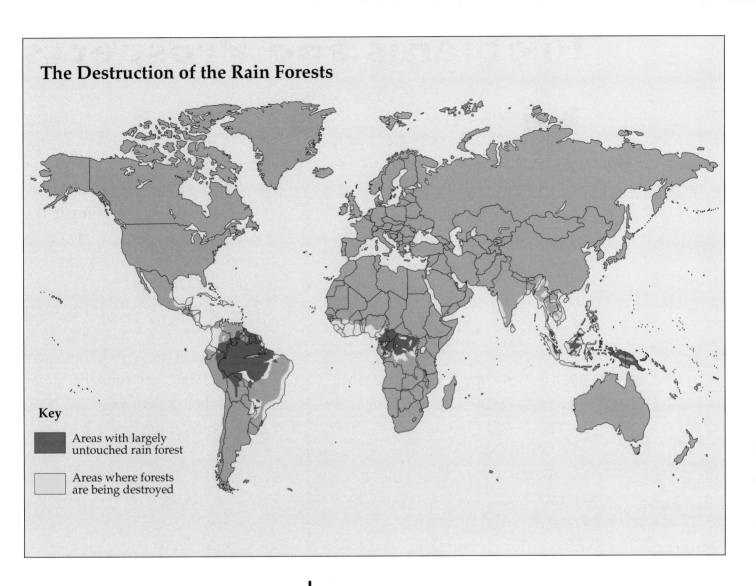

Key

Areas with largely untouched rain forest

Areas where forests are being destroyed

plants and animals will die out and, of course, there will be no more hardwood. To make hardwood available in the future as a resource, the forests must be tended and replanted.

Burning the forests also affects the environment in other ways. For example, it is contributing to the greenhouse effect by producing more carbon dioxide. And it is removing vast expanses of green vegetation, which help the earth breathe by taking in carbon dioxide and giving out oxygen.

Recycling and conservation

We are slowly coming to understand that the world's resources can be used up, and so should be conserved. Materials that we use and throw away are lost forever. It is therefore becoming increasingly important that we recycle the resources we are using, and conserve those that are still unused.

Alloy A mixture of a metal with another metal or with another chemical element.

Casting A method of shaping molten metal in molds.

Catalyst A substance that helps chemical changes take place without being changed itself.

Ceramics Materials produced by baking clay or other earthy materials.

Conductor A substance that passes on heat and electricity well. Metals are good conductors.

Conifer A tree that bears its seeds in cones. Most conifers are evergreen, bearing leaves all year.

Corrode Break down chemically. Iron corrodes in damp air, forming rust.

Deciduous tree One that sheds its leaves in the autumn.

Die A metal mold, used in die-casting.

Ductile A property of a metal that describes how easily it can be stretched without breaking.

Electrolysis Splitting up a compound into its elements by means of electricity.

Elements The basic chemical building blocks that make up matter.

Fiberglass A plastic material containing thin glass fibers, which give it extra strength.

Forging Shaping metal by a hammering action.

Glass Transparent material made mainly from sand and limestone.

Global warming A theory that states that the world's climates will change because the atmosphere is getting warmer (see greenhouse effect).

Greenhouse effect The effect produced by the buildup of certain gases (mainly carbon dioxide) in the atmosphere that prevents heat from escaping the surface of the earth. The atmosphere becomes like a greenhouse, letting the sun's heat in but not letting it out.

Hardwoods Trees whose wood is relatively hard.

Inert Does not combine readily with other substances. The opposite of reactive.

Machining Shaping metals by powered cutting tools called machine tools.

Malleability The ability to be shaped.

Metallurgy The science and technology of metals and metal working.

Mineral A chemical substance found in the earth's crust. Most minerals are compounds containing two or more chemical elements.

Native metal A metal that can be found in its pure state in the earth's crust. Gold and silver are examples.

Ore A mineral containing a metal, and from which the metal can profitably be extracted.

Petrochemicals Chemicals obtained from petroleum, or crude oil.

Plastics Synthetic materials that can be readily molded into shape.

Pollution The poisoning of the land, the water, the air, and the environment in general.

Polymerization A chemical process in which a substance with small molecules is changed into a substance with large ones.

Reactive Combines readily with other substances. The opposite of inert.

Recycling Gathering materials after they have been used once and using them again.

Refining In metallurgy, removing impurities from metals. In the petroleum industry, processing crude oil to produce more useful products.

Refractories Ceramic materials that resist high temperatures.

Rolling Shaping metal by passing it between heavy rollers.

Rubber An elastic material made from the sap of the rubber tree.

Slag The waste material produced during metal smelting that contains impurities.

Smelting Heating metal ores in a furnace to extract the metal.

Softwoods Trees whose wood is relatively soft. They are mostly conifers.

Synthetic Made by humans; not natural.

Synthetic fibers Plastics that can be drawn out into fine fibers and used for making textiles.

Thermoplastics Plastics that soften when reheated.

Thermosets Plastics that set rigid when they form and that cannot be remelted.

Wood pulp Wood fibers, made by shredding or chemically treating wood.

Further Reading

Chandler, Jane. *Glass*. Ada, OK: Garrett Educational Corporation, 1991.

Dyson, Sue. *Wood*. Resources. New York: Thomson Learning, 1993.

Jackman, Wayne. *Plastics*. Resources. New York: Thomson Learning, 1993.

Kerrod, Robin. *Mineral Resources*. World's Resources. New York: Thomson Learning, 1994.

Peacock, Graham. *Bricks*. Resources. New York: Thomson Learning, 1993.

Peckham, Alexander. *Resources Control*. Green Issues. New York: Gloucester Press, 1990.

The Story of Metals. Troy, MI: International Book Center, 1987.

Whyman, Kathryn. *Textiles*. Resources Today. New York: Gloucester Press, 1988.

Picture Acknowledgments

The publishers would like to thank the following for supplying photographs: J. Allan Cash Picture Library, pages 6, 17 right, 18, 20, 22, 27, 30 top, 33, 38 top, 39 both, 41, and 44; Chapel Studios, (Tim Garrod) 33, (Zul Mukhida) 40; Eye Ubiquitous, (Paul Dowd) *cover* cutout, (R..Carroll) 9; GeoScience Features, page 7; Robert Harding Picture Library, pages 26, 37, and 40 both; Hutchison Library, pages 8, 10, and 30 bottom; Science Photo Library, *cover* middle, pages 14, 16, 34, 42 bottom; South American Pictures, (Tony Morrison) pages 21, and 23; Spectrum Colour Library, page 5; Wayland Picture Library, *title page*, pages 12, 13, 17 left, 24, 42 top, and 43; Zefa, *cover* top, *cover* bottom, pages 11, 19, 28 top, and 38 bottom.